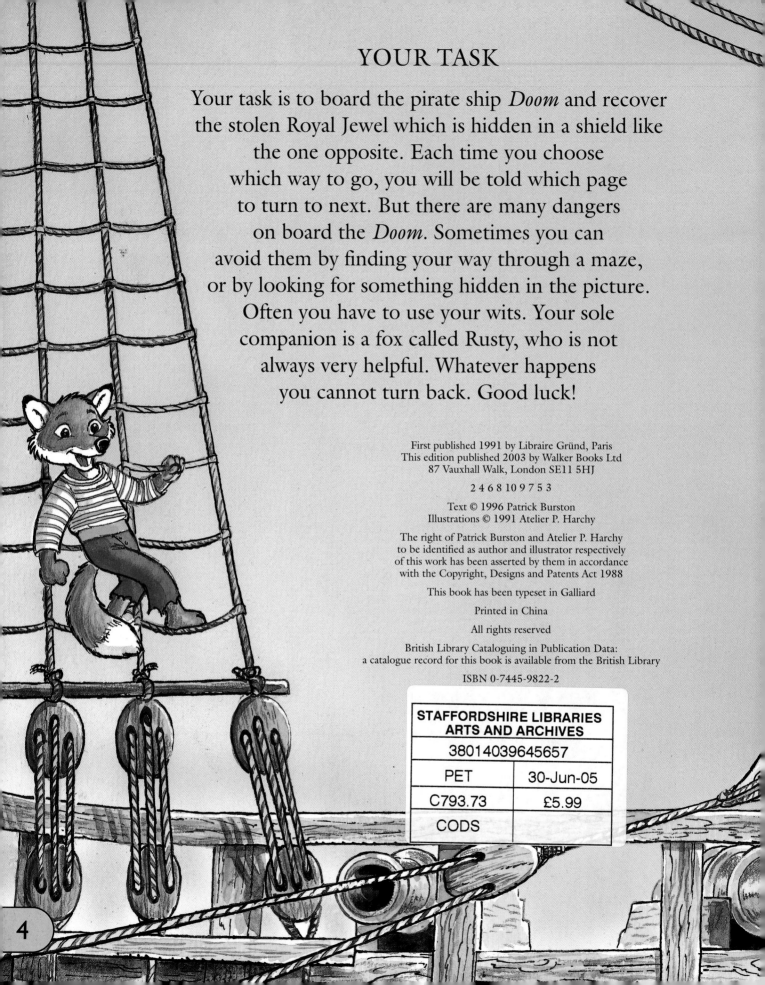

YOUR TASK

Your task is to board the pirate ship *Doom* and recover
the stolen Royal Jewel which is hidden in a shield like
the one opposite. Each time you choose
which way to go, you will be told which page
to turn to next. But there are many dangers
on board the *Doom*. Sometimes you can
avoid them by finding your way through a maze,
or by looking for something hidden in the picture.
Often you have to use your wits. Your sole
companion is a fox called Rusty, who is not
always very helpful. Whatever happens
you cannot turn back. Good luck!

First published 1991 by Libraire Gründ, Paris
This edition published 2003 by Walker Books Ltd
87 Vauxhall Walk, London SE11 5HJ

2 4 6 8 10 9 7 5 3

Text © 1996 Patrick Burston
Illustrations © 1991 Atelier P. Harchy

The right of Patrick Burston and Atelier P. Harchy
to be identified as author and illustrator respectively
of this work has been asserted by them in accordance
with the Copyright, Designs and Patents Act 1988

This book has been typeset in Galliard

Printed in China

All rights reserved

British Library Cataloguing in Publication Data:
a catalogue record for this book is available from the British Library

ISBN 0-7445-9822-2

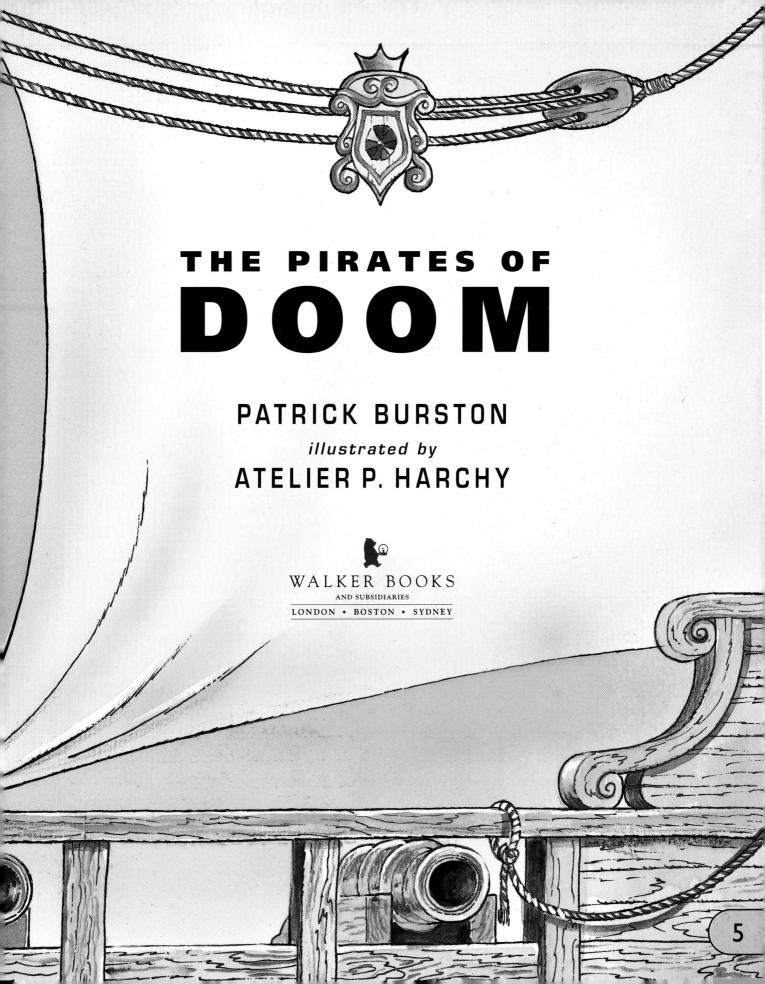

THE PIRATES OF
DOOM

PATRICK BURSTON

illustrated by
ATELIER P. HARCHY

WALKER BOOKS
AND SUBSIDIARIES
LONDON · BOSTON · SYDNEY

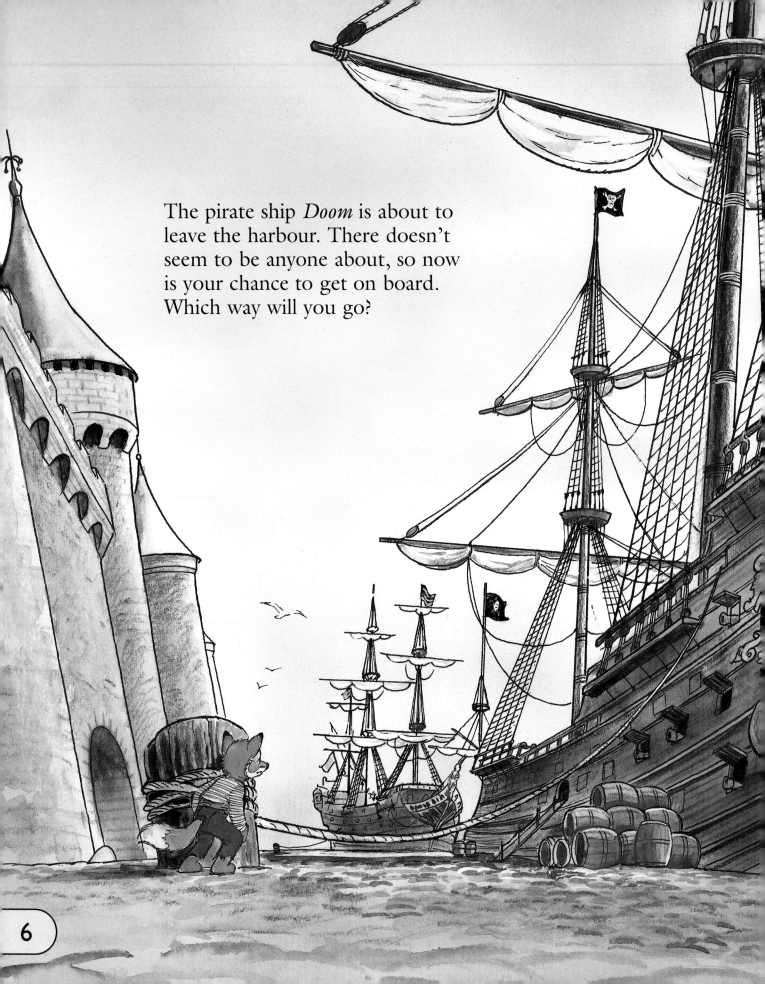

The pirate ship *Doom* is about to
leave the harbour. There doesn't
seem to be anyone about, so now
is your chance to get on board.
Which way will you go?

If you choose to climb
along the rope, turn to
page 10. If you decide
to go up the gangplank,
turn to page 8.

If you go up these steps, turn to page 14.

You are in the ship's hold, where the gunpowder is kept. Five trails of gunpowder have caught fire, but only one of them leads to a gunpowder barrel. Find which one, so that you can save the ship. (Trace each trail with your finger.)

If you go through this door, turn to page 12.

You're on deck, but someone's coming. Find a way to set the cannonballs rolling to trip them up.

If you escape up these steps, turn to page 14.

If you go this way, turn to page 16.

If you climb out of the
window, turn to page 20.

You have to sneak past all the sleeping crew, but don't step on any warped or broken floorboards – they might creak and wake the pirates! (Trace a safe path with your finger.)

If you creep down the stairs, turn to page 18.

13

The ship's wheel has been tied fast with a rope and you are heading for those rocks! Find something shaped like a sword to cut the rope, then steer the ship to safety.

Which way next? You could climb over the side to page 20, or go through the open door to page 22.

The pirates have made stuffed dummies to frighten their enemies, but five of the figures are real! Spot which they are so that you can avoid them.

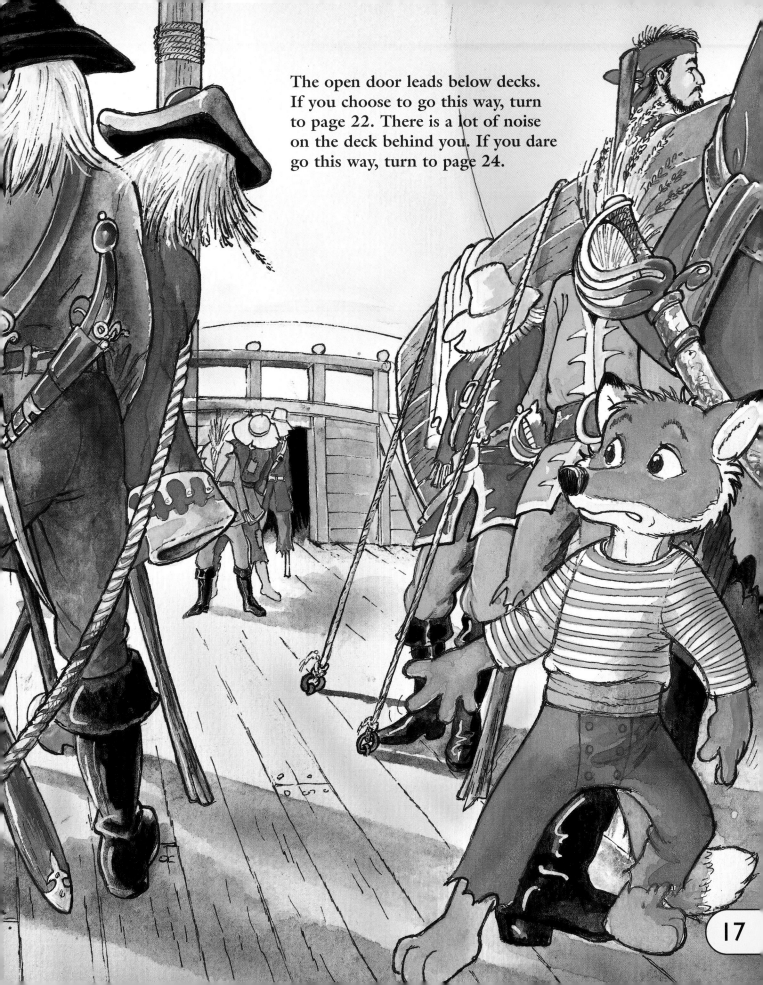

The open door leads below decks. If you choose to go this way, turn to page 22. There is a lot of noise on the deck behind you. If you dare go this way, turn to page 24.

The ship's armoury! Find the five hidden keys so that you can unlock the pirates' weapons and throw them overboard. Then choose which way to go next.

If you go through the door, turn to page 28.

If you choose to go down the steps, turn to page 26.

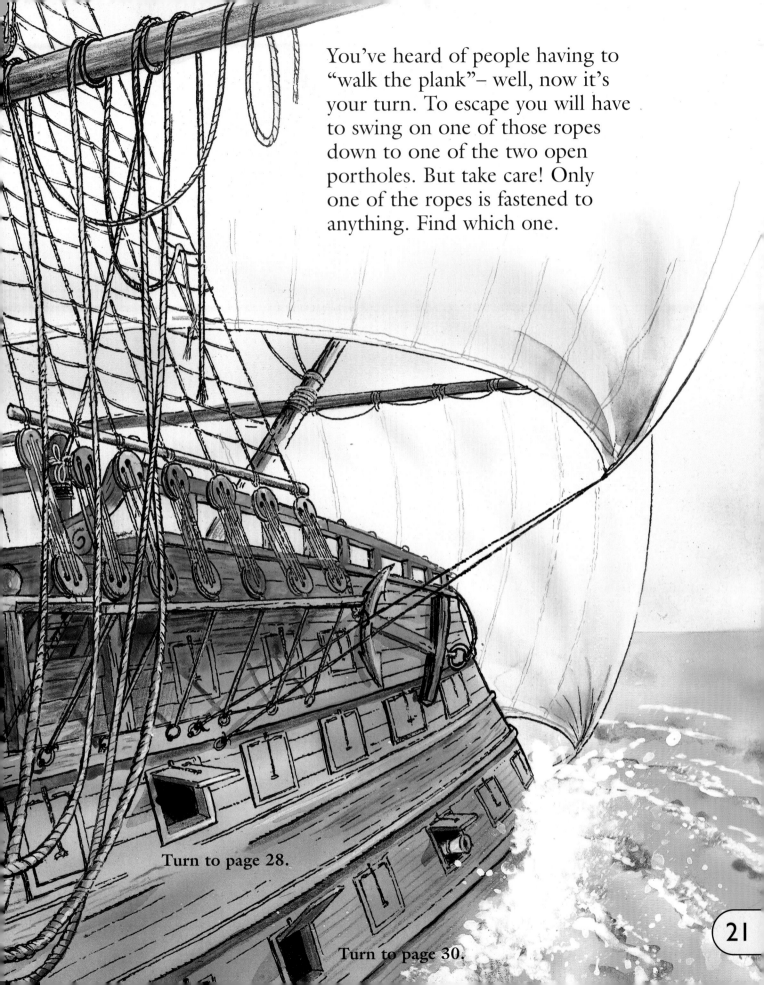

You've heard of people having to "walk the plank"– well, now it's your turn. To escape you will have to swing on one of those ropes down to one of the two open portholes. But take care! Only one of the ropes is fastened to anything. Find which one.

Turn to page 28.

Turn to page 30.

21

If you go through this door, turn to page 32.

You're in the Captain's cabin, and you can hear him behind that screen. Find his wooden leg and throw it out of the porthole so that he can't chase you!

If you decide to go
down these steps,
turn to page 30.

The *Doom* has been boarded by enemy pirates and you're in the thick of the fighting. Count the pirates. If there are the same number with red headbands as there are with black headbands you can escape.

Did you escape? If so, you can use the ladder to go down that open hatch to page 32, or nip up the mast to page 34.

Turn to page 36.

Turn to page 42.

Horrible serpents are lurking in the depths of the ship. Find a way between them through the shallow water. (Trace a path with your finger.) It's safe to cross the ropes.

In the pirates' treasure chamber a magic doll has conjured up an evil spirit. To cancel the spell find another green doll.

Hurry! Choose which way to go!
Out of the porthole to page 36,
or up those steps to page 38.

The cook has spilled flour all over the galley floor. Now he is asleep in the corner. You must creep past him, without stepping in the flour and leaving footprints. (Trace a path with your finger.) You can climb across the furniture if you need to.

Turn to page 38.

Turn to page 40.

The Captain's table is spread with a sumptuous feast. You're hungry, but before you can eat you must spot eight nasty things hiding among the food.

Which way now? To climb
the ladder, turn to page 40.
If you think that parrot
is showing you the way,
turn to page 42.

If you choose this rope, turn to page 42.

You're up in the crow's-nest and the pirates are after you! Find something to hook over one of those two ropes and slide down, but hurry before the albatross returns to protect her chicks!

34

If you choose this rope, turn to page 44.

Beware! Sharks! If you stay close to the ship the outline of a dolphin will scare them off. Can you spot it?

You have failed to find the Royal
Jewel. Swim back to page 6 so you
can try again!

Another pirate ship has moored alongside and only one cannon is pointing at it! Find which fuse will set it off, then light the fuse with the candle.

You still have not
found the Royal Jewel,
so go back to page 6
and try again.

The flame from that lantern has started a fire. You must alert the pirate without him seeing you. Somewhere near Rusty is your loaded catapult. Find it and wake the pirate by firing at the bell above his head.

You have saved the ship, but must go back to page 6 and start again to find the Royal Jewel.

The parrot has torn three maps in half but only the map Rusty's holding will lead you to hidden treasure. Find the other half and you can claim the reward one day. But for now you must return to page 6 and try again to find the Royal Jewel.

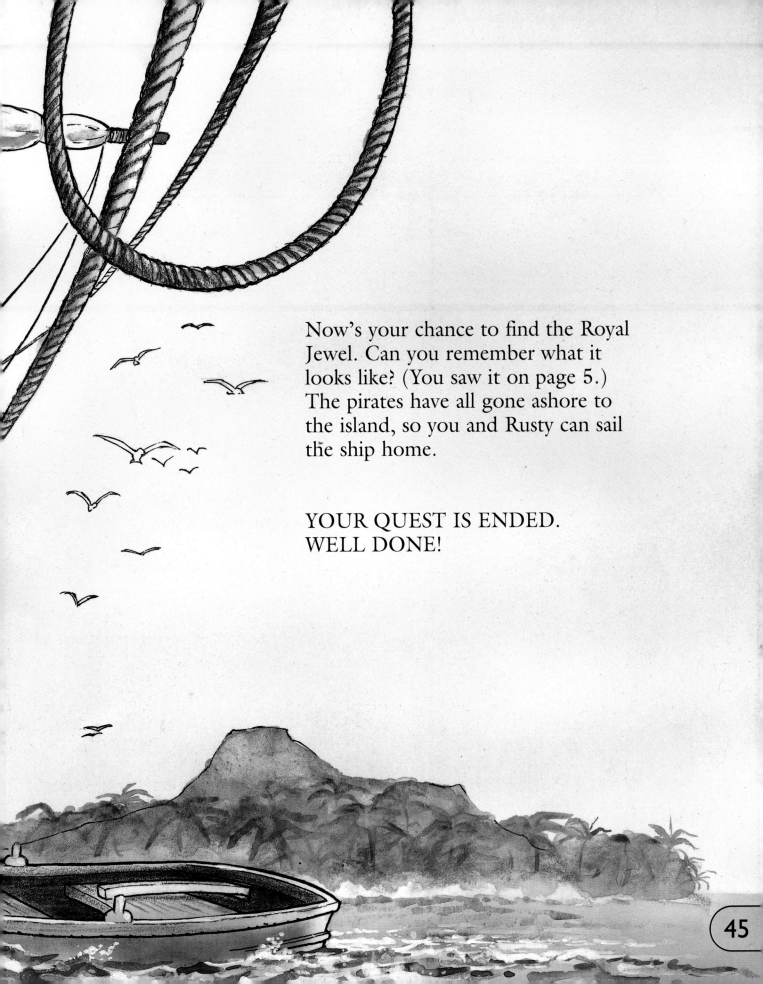

Now's your chance to find the Royal Jewel. Can you remember what it looks like? (You saw it on page 5.) The pirates have all gone ashore to the island, so you and Rusty can sail the ship home.

YOUR QUEST IS ENDED.
WELL DONE!

Answers

10
pull the rope to send the
cannonballs rolling in all directions

14
you can use the swordfish on the
wall to cut the rope

24
there are equal numbers of pirates
with red headbands and black
headbands – 15 of each

32
- a caterpillar in the lettuce
- a crab among the pineapples
- a grub in the mangoes
- a red spider on the tomatoes
- a snake among the cucumbers
- a centipede under the napkin
- a tentacle reaching from the jug
- a bee in the honeypot

34
use the pirate's hook

36
the dolphin outline is on the hull of the ship

40
the catapult is lying in the rope behind Rusty